Charge into Reading

Decodable Reader
with literacy activities

Run, Pug!
Short U

Brooke Vitale • Katarzyna Jasinska

CHARGE MOMMY
BOOKS
Riverside, CT

Copyright © 2022 Charge Mommy Books, LLC. All rights reserved.

No part of this book may be reproduced or transmitted in any form or by any means, electronic or mechanical, including photocopying, recording, or by any information storage and retrieval system, without written permission from the publisher.

For information address contact@chargemommybooks.com
or visit chargemommybooks.com.

Printed in China
ISBN: 978-1-955947-21-3
10 9 8 7

Designed by Lindsay Broderick
Created in consultation with literacy specialist Marisa Ware, MSEd

Publisher's Cataloging-in-Publication Data
Names: Vitale, Brooke, author. | Jasinska, Katarzyna, illustrator.
Title: Run, pug! : short u decodable reader / Brooke Vitale, Katarzyna Jasinska.
Description: Riverside, CT : Charge Mommy Books, 2022.| Illustrated early reader. | Series: Charge into Reading. | Audience: Ages 4-6. | Summary: Introduces children to the short U sound. Includes eight pages of short U literacy activities at the end.
Identifiers: LCCN 2022901779 | ISBN 9781955947213 (pbk.)
Subjects: LCSH: Dogs -- Juvenile fiction. | Reading -- Code emphasis approaches -- Juvenile literature. | Reading -- Phonetic method -- Juvenile literature. | Readers (Primary). | BISAC: JUVENILE FICTION / Animals / Dogs. | JUVENILE FICTION / Concepts / Sounds. | JUVENILE FICTION / Readers / Beginner.
Classification: LCC PZ7.1 V59 Run 2022 | DDC E V59ru--dc22
LC record available at https://lccn.loc.gov/2022901779

Gus is a pug.

Gus tugs a mug.

Gus tugs a rug.

Gus is in luck.

Bugs!

Gus runs.

The bugs run.

The bugs run in the sun.

Gus runs in the sun.

The bugs run in the mud.

Gus runs in the mud.

The bugs run in a hut.

Gus runs in the hut.

Bugs. Yum!

Let's Talk Literacy!

Read the sentence below. Then circle the picture that matches the sentence.

Gus runs in the mud.

Let's Talk Literacy!

Say the name of each picture below. As you speak, **tap out** the sounds for each word. Then **write the letter** for each sound in the box.

Answers: m-u-g / s-u-n / b-u-s

Let's Talk Literacy!

Say the name of each picture below. Then circle the words that make a **short U sound**.

Answers: gum, bug, cup, jug, rug

Let's Talk Literacy!

Say the name of the picture in each row. Then circle the word in each row that is part of the same **word family**.

tub

tun nut sub bud hum

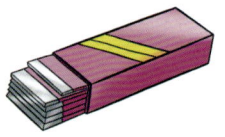
gum

mud sum gut tug mug

nut

pun but lug dud tub

Let's Talk Literacy!

Say the word. Then look at the picture to figure out its **rhyming word**. Change the first letter of the word to make the new word, and write it on the line.

Word	Change to	New word
lug	🐞	_____
fun	☀️	_____
cut	🌰	_____

Let's Talk Literacy!

Look at each picture below. Then read the words below each picture. **Circle the word** that matches the picture.

bun bus but

sun fun sub

gut hum gum

mug hug mud

pub bug pug

sun sub rub

Let's Talk Literacy!

The word **hug** is part of the **-UG word family**. Name the pictures below. Then circle the ones that are also part of the -UG word family.

Answers: pug, mug, jug, rug, bug

Let's Talk Literacy!

Say the name of each picture below. Then draw a line to the letter that makes the **first sound** in the word.

Gg　Dd　Tt　Bb　Ss　Rr

  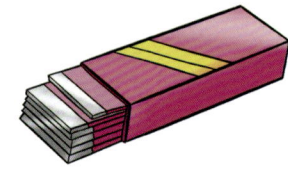